WEST AFRICAN KINGDOMS
EMPIRES OF GOLD AND TRADE

by
KATHERINE REECE

Rourke
Publishing LLC
Vero Beach, Florida 32964

www.rourkepublishing.com

PHOTO CREDITS:
Courtesy www.bigfoto.com: Cover, page 7; Courtesy www.classiccrossstitch.com: page 13; Courtesy Charles Reasoner: pages 10, 18, 22, 25, 27; Courtesy Corel Stock Photos: Title, pages 8, 12, 14, 16, 20, 26, 28, 29, 31, 34, 35, 37, 38, 43, 45; Courtesy www.desertvoice.net: page 32; Courtesy www.laurelschool.net: page 24; Courtesy Library of Congress, Prints and Photographs Division: pages 4, 15, 19, 30; Courtesy NASA: page 5; Courtesy www.playahata.com: page 33; Courtesy Rohm Padilla: pages 6, 11.

DESIGN AND LAYOUT: ROHM PADILLA
RESEARCH/PAGINATION: SANDY HUGHES

Library of Congress Cataloging-in-Publication Data

Reece, Katherine E., 1955-
    West African Kingdoms: empires of gold and trade / Katherine Reece.
            p. c.m. -- (Ancient Civilizations)
    Includes bibliographical references and index.
    ISBN 1-59515-508-2 (hardcover)

TITLE PAGE IMAGE
West African Muslims in front of a mosque in Mali

Printed in the USA.

TABLE OF CONTENTS

INTRODUCTION ... 4

Chapter I
WHERE WERE THE WEST AFRICAN KINGDOMS? ... 5

Chapter II
WHO WERE THE WEST AFRICANS? ... 8

Chapter III
WHAT DID WEST AFRICANS EAT? ... 28

Chapter IV
WHAT DID WEST AFRICANS WEAR? ... 30

Chapter V
TRADE AND COMMERCE ... 32

Chapter VI
ART AND ARCHITECTURE ... 35

Chapter VII
BELIEFS AND GODS ... 38

Chapter VIII
THE PEOPLE TODAY ... 41

A Timeline of the History of the West African Kingdoms ... 44
Glossary ... 46
Books of Interest ... 47
Web Sites ... 47
Index ... 48

INTRODUCTION

Jesse Owens, an Olympic runner, begins a race.

Do you wrestle or enjoy running? Are you amazed at the skill of a **discus** or **javelin** thrower in Olympic Games? These sports, and even simple games like hopscotch or tic-tac-toe, began centuries ago in West Africa. In ancient times, the sports not only were fun, but also developed a warrior's skills for battle.

From 500 to 1700 **C.E.**, three great kingdoms known for their gold trade and education centers formed in West Africa. As one kingdom ended, another took its place. Ghana, Mali, and Songhay became famous for their art, science, education, trade, government, and warfare.

CHAPTER 1:
WHERE WERE THE WEST AFRICAN KINGDOMS?

West Africa stretched from the Atlantic coast eastward in a strip between the **Sahara** Desert to the north and the rain forest to the south. The area remained undiscovered and wrapped in mystery for centuries because it was difficult to cross such a vast ocean of sand.

Arabs called this region **Sahel**, meaning "shore," since it formed a border along the Sahara Desert. The Kingdoms of Ghana, Mali, and Songhay occupied an important location for trade across northern Africa. Early villages began in places where people could find water and grow crops important for survival and later for trade.

An aerial view of the central Sahara Desert

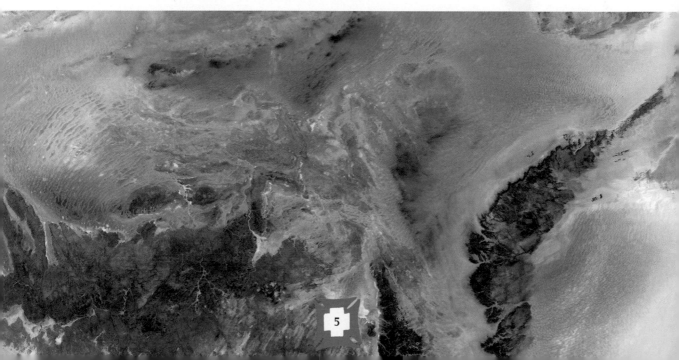

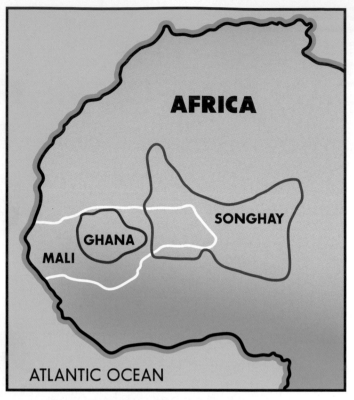

Location of the ancient West African kingdoms of Ghana, Songhay, and Mali

The **Kingdom of Ghana** originated with the **Soninke** clan and lasted from 700 C.E. until 1076 C.E. in an area approximately 500 miles (805 km) north of present-day Ghana. At the height of its power, the kingdom covered 250,000 square miles (647,450 sq km), an area about as large as the state of Texas! The kingdom was situated between the Niger and Senegal rivers and included what is now western Mali, Senegal, and southeast Mauritania.

The **Kingdom of Mali** occupied all of Ghana's borders and expanded west to the Atlantic Ocean. Its northern border included parts of the Sahara Desert, and in the south it extended down the Niger River, past the city of Djenne. To the east, the kingdom stretched to the city of Takrur. The **empire** covered 2,000 miles (3,200 km) from the Atlantic Ocean in the west to beyond Gao in the east, and from the southern edge of the Sahara to the forest belt in the south.

The **Kingdom of Songhay** had its beginnings at Gao, near the bend of the Niger River. Its borders today would include modern Mali, Niger, Benin, Burkina Faso, Gambia, Guinea, Mauritania, and Senegal.

West African kingdoms contained diverse geography, plants, animals, peoples, languages, and cultures. Dust storms were common in the hot, dry desert areas, where temperatures could fall from 100° F (38° C) during the day to 45° F (7° C) at night. Flood waters from the Niger River affected the middle of the Sahel and made it possible to grow crops. Most of the year rainfall was irregular, but 15.75 inches (40 cm) to 23.62 inches (60 cm) of rain fell during the rainy season between July and September. Droughts in the area dried the river, causing famines and the declines of empires. Southern areas contained drought-resistant tall grasses and scattered trees and bushes. A rain forest, rich with tropical wildlife, plants and crops of **kola nuts** and **plantain**, was further south. Dolphins and **manatees** swam along the Atlantic coast.

A monkey eating a piece of fruit, Ghana

CHAPTER II:

WHO WERE THE WEST AFRICANS?

Clans were very important to the structure of the West African family and village. Each person belonged to a clan, and each clan had a special job. Most people were farmers who lived in clusters of small, round houses made of mud or stone connected to each other. The homes had domed grass roofs. A short wall surrounded their homes for protection from wild animals. Inside was a cot or sleeping mat for each person, rugs to cover the dirt floors, a few wooden stools, and candles for light. Very little furniture was necessary since most activities were outside.

Many houses were made of mud, and some buildings had grass roofs.

Men and women worked hard. Children learned life's skills by following their parents' footsteps. Men farmed, hunted, fished, and served in the king's army. Women weeded the gardens, tended the vegetables, prepared the family meals, and made clay pottery. Everyone joined in the harvest. West African children were raised by their mothers until they were 12 years old. Then boys went to study with their uncles, and girls married and began raising their own families.

A boy carrying a baby on his back

The history of West Africans was passed down to children by village storytellers called **griots**. Griots kept the past alive through their storytelling since there were no written records. Griots memorized long **epics** and told the stories as they danced, sang, or played music. Every clan and every king had a griot. For the king, griots were official record keepers and some became advisers to the king.

CLANS

West Africans come from many clans with thousands of different languages. Each clan is headed by the oldest male member and has a special task it does such as metalwork, fishing, or providing leaders and kings. Children are prized, and a great celebration is held for new babies.

A Berber warrior

Clans joined together to form villages, each with its own ruler. As a ruler gained power, he united villages into kingdoms. West African leaders who were strong conquered and combined kingdoms to form even larger empires.

The Kingdom of Ghana had been ruled by more than 40 kings by 300 C.E. Early Ghanaians were peaceful and lived by farming and mining. Between 300 C.E. and 770 C.E., **Berbers** ruled the Kingdom of Ghana. Around 700 C.E. a group of Soninke, who lived northwest of the great bend in the Niger River, founded the state of Wagadou. This became an **oasis** along an important trade route where gold and ivory from the south were exchanged for salt from the desert to the north. The Soninke forced the Berbers out of the region, and the empire of Ghana expanded. This marked the beginning of trade beyond their region.

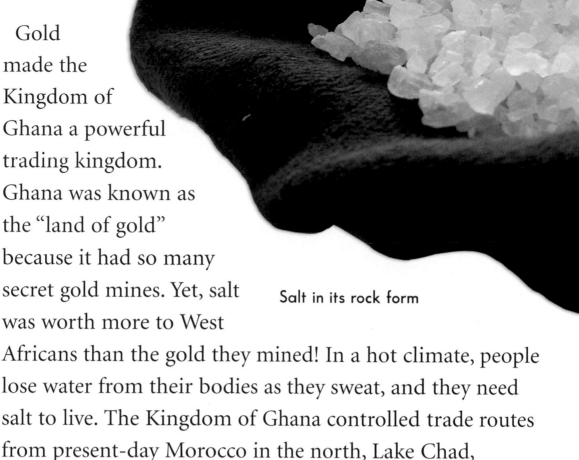

Gold made the Kingdom of Ghana a powerful trading kingdom. Ghana was known as the "land of gold" because it had so many secret gold mines. Yet, salt

Salt in its rock form

was worth more to West Africans than the gold they mined! In a hot climate, people lose water from their bodies as they sweat, and they need salt to live. The Kingdom of Ghana controlled trade routes from present-day Morocco in the north, Lake Chad, Nubia/Egypt in the east, and the coastal forests of western Africa in the south.

The Soninke founded the capital city of Kumbi Saleh, where more than 30,000 people lived. The city was divided into two towns that were about 6 miles (9.6 km) apart. One town was for the ruler and native Western African people who still worshiped their own gods. A thick wall surrounded the king's half of Kumbi Saleh. Inside the wall, the king's large house was surrounded by smaller homes for his wives, children, and government workers.

Muslim traders, lawyers, religious leaders, and teachers lived in the other town of Kumbi Saleh in two-story, mud-brick homes with flat roofs. The ground floor was used for storage, and the families lived upstairs. There were 12 **mosques** throughout Kumbi Saleh. A large open market bustled with activity as people gathered to trade horses, cloth, swords, books, jewelry, silk, and even rare birds.

The **Kante** clan, who specialized as blacksmiths, made farming tools and weapons of iron that increased Ghana's wealth and power. With the new tools, farmers could produce enough food for their families and harvest extra crops to sell or trade. Surrounding kingdoms were taken over by the Kingdom of Ghana with its huge armies of up to 200,000 men! Neighboring villages with their weapons of stone, bone, and wood were no match against warriors carrying spears tipped with iron.

Horses have been traded and sold for centuries.

Another reason for the growth of West African kingdoms was their use of camels and horses. Trade across the Sahara Desert was possible because camels could withstand the desert heat and go for days without water. Warriors with horses were superior to foot soldiers in the lands they conquered.

The Ghana king was more powerful than anyone and considered to be the father of all Soninke people. He was the religious leader, chief of the army, and highest judge. His people worshiped and served him like a god. Special drummers followed the king around. When he appeared in public, his subjects would lie on the ground and throw dust on their heads. The king controlled all the gold that was mined in his kingdom and began a system of **tributes**.

Caravans of camels transported many trade goods including food and gold.

THE HARDIEST ANIMAL ON EARTH

Camels can drink more than 26 gallons (100 liters) of water at one time and go up to nine days without drinking again. They do not perspire, so valuable moisture is not lost. They can fill up on food and then live off body fat without losing any muscle. Add the fact they can carry more than 330 lb (150 kg) of goods on their backs, and they are truly hardy animals!

As the kingdom grew, a more organized government was needed. Three independent states called Mali, Mema, and Wagadou were formed. These were separated into 12 **provinces**, each with its own governor and protected by troops. Local rulers were left in charge of newly conquered lands, but their people were expected to obey the king and pay tribute to the Kingdom of Ghana.

Camels loading up on water

The great wealth of the Kingdom of Ghana weakened during a seven-year period of droughts. Crops died and famine spread throughout the kingdom. The king was no longer powerful enough to control the salt and gold trade. Areas broke up into smaller kingdoms that began to fight among each other for power.

Weakened from within, the Kingdom of Ghana was open to attack. Around 1054 C.E., Muslim warriors from Morocco called Almoravids conquered the Kingdom of Ghana. They taught **Islam** to the people. Arabic, the language of the **Koran** (Qur'an), became the common language of the traders and merchants of Ghana. Reading and writing spread throughout the country because belief in Islam required everyone to learn the Koran.

A West African leader and his assembly in Ghana, 1972

Many farms lie along the Niger River.

More than 150 years passed before the kingdoms were united again. Sundiata Keita, a **Mandinka** ruler, built a new empire known as the Kingdom of Mali in 1235 C.E. From the capital city of Niani on the Niger River, Sundiata expanded his kingdom to include lands in the Kingdom of Ghana plus more territory. The Kingdom of Mali was three times the size of former Ghana. Mali was so large that it took four months to travel across the kingdom by donkey or camel! With the empire close to the gold mines in West Africa and fertile interior plains of the Niger River, the Kingdom of Mali was the richest country of its day.

ISLAM

Islam is a religion founded by the prophet **Muhammad** who was born in 570 C.E. People who practice Islam are called Muslims and worship only one god, **Allah**. Islam is spread by those who practice the religion and by holy war, called a **jihad**.

Trade and military power held the empire and government together. Mali's horsemen were armed with steel armor, spears, and iron swords. The Kingdom of Mali controlled the gold trade from 1235 to 1500 C.E. and managed the salt trade in the north. Trade routes expanded, and **caravans** traveled as far east as Egypt to trade for copper.

Arabic writing from the Koran

King Sundiata used his armies to protect all trade routes so that Muslim traders felt safe again. In return, traders paid **tariffs** to Sundiata for every load of goods they carried. Armies cleared land and planted crops near the Niger River, and Mali's farms provided more food than Ghana's. Food was shipped on the Niger River from the farms to the cities.

The title of king was passed from the king to his son, or to the son of the king's sister. All kings were called mansas, which means "lord" in the Mandinka language. Like Ghana, Mali was divided into provinces with governors in charge. Advisers were in charge of specific areas such as fishing or farming and helped the Mali mansas rule.

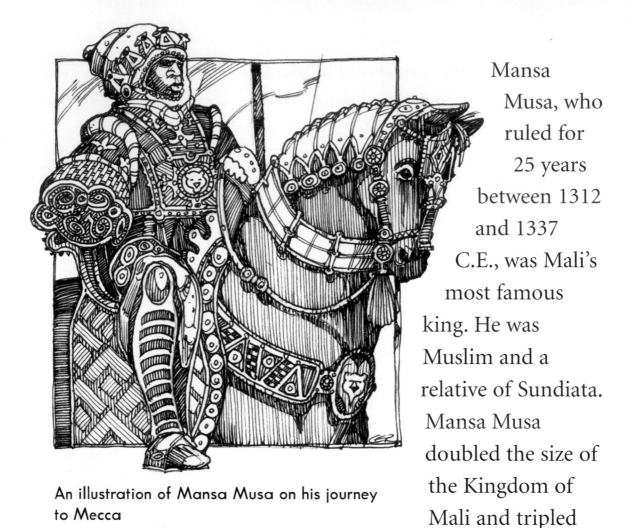

Mansa Musa, who ruled for 25 years between 1312 and 1337 C.E., was Mali's most famous king. He was Muslim and a relative of Sundiata. Mansa Musa doubled the size of the Kingdom of Mali and tripled the amount of trade. His advisers regulated fishing on the Niger River and travel through the forests, as well as increased profits from agriculture, tariffs, and tributes.

An illustration of Mansa Musa on his journey to Mecca

Mansa Musa is remembered for his **pilgrimage**, or **hajj**, to the city of **Mecca** in present-day Saudi Arabia in 1325 C.E. He brought back new ideas, teachers, writers, scientists, and builders from Egypt. Large mosques, state courts of law, and famous schools were built in Timbuktu, Djenne, and Gao.

Ideas of religion, mathematics, law, and literature were taught and exchanged. Personal libraries of the rich could contain more than 15,000 books! Courts of law applied the teachings of the Koran to everyday life. Islam was becoming well established, but native West Africans still practiced their personal religions.

View of tent city outside Kaaba, Mecca

MANSA MUSA TO MECCA

It is estimated that 60,000 people including princes and army leaders traveled with Mansa Musa to Mecca. Some think Musa took the princes and army leaders so they could not take over his kingdom while he was away. About 500 slaves, carrying staffs of pure gold, were a part of the large group of people with the king. About 80 camels carried 300 lb (136 kg) of gold each. Others carried food, clothing, and supplies. It is said Musa's generosity was so great that he gave away all his gold and had to borrow money for his return to Mali.

The king's overspending nearly brought Mali to an end. Mansa Musa died in 1337 C.E., and his son became king. He was not strong like his father, and individual kingdoms became self governing again. Over the next 200 years, the empire grew smaller and smaller until only the city of Niani remained. The Kingdom of Mali had ended.

The Kingdom of Songhay had its beginnings as early as 800 C.E. when the Songhay clan built their capital city in Gao. The city was located in fertile grasslands in the heart of the Sahara Desert trade routes. These important trade routes connected North Africa and Arabia to the forest regions of the south.

The Songhay enjoyed a high standard of living. The Niger River was good for fishing and supplied water for farming. Songhay trade routes between the regions up and down the river supplied all that the people needed.

Washing clothes in the Niger River

The Songhay people were divided into very distinct classes. Nobility included members of the ruling family and merchants. Next were the freemen and craftsmen, and below them were the peasants and slaves. Peasants and slaves, captured in wars, were poor, lived in the countryside, and worked on the royal estates.

Trade with the Arabs brought the teachings of Islam to the region. Around 1009 C.E. King Kossoi was the first Songhay ruler to accept Islam. He recognized that the religion of the Muslim merchants would be good for trade, and increased trade would make him more powerful. Islam helped to unite the people, and Islamic traditions and beliefs influenced governmental decisions. King Kossoi adopted other useful ideas such as the **shaduf**, a hoist for irrigation used on the Nile River, the use of animal waste for fertilizer on crops, and the milking of cattle.

As the Kingdom of Mali was growing weaker, Gao grew stronger. The city had been invaded by Mansa Musa in 1325 C.E. After Mansa Musa died in 1346 C.E., a Songhay prince returned home to free his people. In 1400 C.E., the Songhay raided Niani, the Mali capital.

King Sonni Ali came to power in 1463 C.E. and is credited with founding the Kingdom of Songhay. Sonni Ali was courageous, intelligent, and insisted that his rules be obeyed. He knew the importance of the Niger River as a means of transportation, but also organized the boatmen of the Niger River to form a professional navy. With a strong army and navy, Sonni Ali built the largest empire in Africa, making the Kingdom of Songhay the most powerful state in West Africa. His kingdom included all the lands occupied by the Soninke of Ghana and the Mandinka in Mali and extended further east and north.

King Sonni Ali

King Sonni Ali accepted Islam and even took a Muslim name. However, he did not forget his native ways and refused to give absolute loyalty to Islam. Timbuktu and Djenne were important centers of learning and trade during the Kingdom of Mali. People from as far away as India even came to Timbuktu to study! As king, Sonni Ali seized the cities and killed Muslim scholars who did not like his native religion. He captured Djenne even though it took him seven years, seven months, and seven days.

King Sonni Ali was determined to build an empire that was peaceful and stable. He needed a system for bringing the different clans and kingdoms together. He placed trusted governors in the provinces and used his army to maintain law and order. Sonni also allowed local leaders to stay in power in the countries he conquered and collected tributes from them.

GREAT WARRIOR

King Sonni Ali was known as a great warrior who was thought to have magical powers and is remembered by historians as "always the conqueror, never the conquered." He was thought to have magic charms called **korte**, which made his soldiers and horses invisible and gave them the power to fly! Sonni himself was thought to be able to change into a vulture.

In 1493 C.E. Mohammed Askia, who had once been Sonni Ali's general, became king. Mohammed completely embraced Islam for himself and in all that he did as a ruler. He understood that the wealth of his kingdom depended on the activities of the Muslim traders. Rural areas may have kept their own beliefs, but the daily work of the kingdom was based on Islamic traditions and beliefs.

King Mohammed Askia appointed Islamic judges who made decisions based on Muslim law. Askia made laws against cheating in business, which were enforced by his royal officers. Muslim laws gave every member of each clan equal rights. Instead of positions being passed from father to son, now anyone could advance in government or status based on his own work.

Muslim women in traditional dress

TRADITIONS AND BELIEFS OF ISLAM

Muslims pray five times each day and fast during the month of **Ramadan**. They are required to give offerings. Women practice **purdah**, which means they stay in a section of the house away from strangers and cover their heads and faces if they leave the home.

Mohammed Askia encouraged schooling and pilgrimage to Mecca. His own hajj resulted in good relations between the Middle East and Songhay and attracted many famous scholars. Askia built more than 180 Koranic schools in Timbuktu where elementary and primary students were taught to read and recite the Koran. Students also learned theology, traditions of Islamic law, grammar, astrology, and history.

King Mohammed
Askia

Mohammed Askia expanded the Kingdom of Songhay from the Atlantic coast to include what is now central Nigeria. He divided the kingdom into five regions, each ruled by a governor. The regions were further divided into provinces ruled by administrators. Like kings before him, he was surrounded by his advisers on military, farming, fishing, forests, and property.

King Askia had royal estates throughout his kingdom that produced crops to feed the people and his military, and for trade. Anyone could farm by renting land at reasonable prices from landowners. In fact, people often left their work during the growing season because they could make more money on the farms. Slaves were used to work on the royal estates where they grew crops, fished, and made **sorghum**. Craftsmen on these estates made tools, spears, and arrows for the military.

Farming was profitable during the growing season.

Mohammed Askia's army was the largest force in Western Africa with over 30,000 foot soldiers and 10,000 horsemen. Armed with lances, swords, bows and arrows, and iron breastplates, only the kings and nobles rode horses. The infantry, or foot soldiers, were made up of lesser nobility, slaves, and peasants. They carried spears, bows and arrows, and wore leather or copper breastplates.

Leather shields would be painted and decorated.

As powerful as they were with their iron spears, the Songhay were no match for an early version of a gun, called a harquebus. **Moors** from Morocco invaded and conquered the Kingdom of Songhay with their guns and cannons in 1600 C.E. When the Moors could not find the secret gold mines, they robbed the Songhay people and tore down many of their towns.

The Kingdom of Songhay was now poor and divided. The people could not continue the salt and gold trade. With no armies to protect them, merchants were robbed by thieves along the trade routes. No trade meant no tariffs, and the West African kingdoms were over.

CHAPTER III:

WHAT DID WEST AFRICANS EAT?

West Africans grew and ate yams, plantains, and other vegetables and fruits like pumpkins and watermelons. Common foods of their diet included grains such as millet, rice, sorghum, and **monkey bread**. Occasionally they ate meat from the large number of animals that roamed their land such as giraffes, lions, elephants, crocodiles, and hippopotamuses. Fish were taken from the Niger River. Many varieties of birds, nesting along the riverbanks, provided meat and eggs.

Gardeners inspecting a stalk of sorghum

The merchants, traders, and nobles who lived in the cities had more variety in their diet. Their tables were often set with beef, lamb, and chicken. They served their guests green peppers stuffed with rice, milk, fruit, and meat.

A woman and child at a local market in Ghana

Salt was an extremely important part of the diet for West Africans since it helped them retain body moisture. Salt was also needed to preserve foods and add flavor to meals.

MONKEY BREAD

African baobab trees grow very large and look like they have roots for branches. Their thick trunks provide homes for many animals. The West Africans collect rainwater from the trunks and use the leaves to make sauces for food or to heal wounds. The gourd-shaped pods of the tree have seeds that can be eaten or made into a drink. This pulp is called monkey bread since monkeys eat it too! Empty pods are used for cups and bowls.

CHAPTER IV:

WHAT DID WEST AFRICANS WEAR?

West Africans made their clothing by weaving plant fibers from cotton that they grew. The skins of animals also provided covering. Clothing was simple, loose, and light because of the heat. Many wore cloths over their faces for protection against dust storms.

Both men and women wrapped pieces of cotton cloth around their bodies. The women fashioned slings with their clothing in order to carry their babies. This kept their hands free for making pottery or working in the fields. Women also twisted and wrapped colorful pieces of cloth into **turbans** for their heads. Children's clothing was cloth wrapped around the waist. People either went barefoot or wore simple sandals.

A father and son from Timbuktu in traditional dress

30

Clothing indicated social status, and in the cities like Timbuktu the women dressed more luxuriously. They were fond of jewels and decorated their hair with bands of gold. Elaborate headdresses and skirts of feathers were made for special ceremonies. Kings were the only people with sewn clothing, and their colorful garments were made with real gold threads!

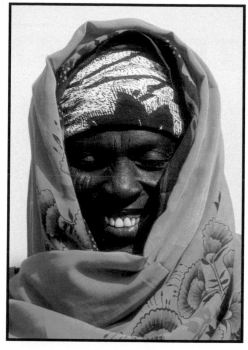

A woman in traditional dress (above) and young women in decorative dress (below)

CHAPTER V:
TRADE AND COMMERCE

The location of West African kingdoms on the "shore" of the Sahara Desert made it possible for them to profit from trade between the northern section and the rest of Africa. Salt from Taghaza, north of Ghana, was traded for gold mined in Bambuk, south of Ghana.

Caravans from as far away as China crossed the desert in order to trade their goods with the West African kingdoms. Camels carried loads of copper from Mali, ivory from the grasslands and rain forests, honey, dried fruit, kola nuts, food, jewelry, leather goods, and slaves from the West African kingdoms to Europe, Egypt, and the Middle East. They returned with ornaments, jewels, clothing, silk, sugar, glassware, minerals, weapons, and fine tools.

A trade caravan in the Sahara Desert

At first one kind of item was traded for another, but traders began to use **cowrie** shells as a form of money. Because salt was so valuable, it was traded pound for pound for gold!

Merchants used scales to weigh their gold or precious stones for payment.

Gold dust was used to pay for goods, and eventually gold **dinars** made from the gold taken to Europe and Arabia replaced cowrie shells.

Example of a gold nugget

SECRET MINES

In order to keep the location of the gold mines secret, a separate meeting place was used in trading. Traders placed their goods on the ground, beat a drum, and then left the area. After hearing the drum, miners brought their gold, beat the drum to signal the trade, and left. The traders came back, and if there was enough gold dust there, they took it and left. If they wanted more, they beat the drum again. The miners came back and left more gold, or decided against the trade and left.

Control of the Niger River was important for trade and travel and provided the route for conquering lands downstream. Large fallen trees were hollowed out and used to make canoes. Sometimes two smaller trees were tied together with cord to make a type of raft still used today.

By the 1400s Timbuktu, Gao, and Djenne were major centers of trade. In Timbuktu weavers, tailors, tanners, shoemakers, goldsmiths, potters, salt makers, and makers of weapons and farming tools provided many items for trade. On the bend of the Niger River, Gao farmers and fishermen produced crops and filled the markets with fish. Djenne was close to the rain forest region and was the first point of exchange for traders to the south.

A market outside the Djenne mosque, Mali

CHAPTER VI:
ART AND ARCHITECTURE

West Africans felt that being creative was a gift from the gods. Weavers of cloth and blacksmiths were both honored and feared. Blacksmiths were believed to have a magical skill that was passed from fathers to their sons. How else could they take a stone containing iron and apply fire and air

A design on a brass lid from Ghana

to make tools and weapons? West Africans believed spiders were sent by the gods to teach people the magic of weaving.

Women wove fabric from cotton and made clothing, sandals, pottery, and jewelry. Men made bows, arrows, spears, hoes, axes, and other tools. Both worked to craft baskets, pots, and utensils. Pottery was decorated with **geometric** pictures in the shapes of animals and other symbols to show daily life and religious beliefs.

Men making rope

Musical instruments made of simple materials were created for ceremonies, dance, and storytelling. West Africans hollowed out gourds for an early instrument called a **balaphon**. They made drums from wood covered with animal skins. Even a small type of handheld piano was made by attaching metal or wooden strips to a sounding board.

An instrument made out of a hollowed-out gourd

Griots were responsible for any record of the past until Muslim traders and Islam brought scholars and writing. Most written records by traders show the effect of Islam on Africa in the Koran. The well-known story of Sundiata Keita, the lion king, which was passed down by griots, was finally recorded on the written page.

THE LION KING

The Epic of Sundiata tells the story of a small boy who overcame his health problems and enemies to become a great and powerful king. Prince Sundiata was born very sick and for years was unable to walk or even stand. Sundiata's half brother took over the throne after their father's death and forced Sundiata to leave the country. While away, Sundiata learned to walk and became a skilled warrior. He formed a large army and overthrew his cruel brother to become the king of Mali.

Muslims built mosques in the cities for worship. Early mosques were made from dried earth and decorated with wooden projections, or **minarets**, and patterns in clay. From the high tower, Muslims were called to their daily prayers. The towers were actually a mix of Islamic belief and native tradition, since the same types of towers were used as ancestor markers in the Kingdom of Songhay.

Mosques such as this one in Timbuktu show a combination of Islamic belief and native traditions.

CHAPTER VII:
BELIEFS AND GODS

Religion shaped the early West African kingdoms. The different clans worshiped many gods, goddesses, and objects such as trees, rocks, and animals. Staying in harmony with nature and the gods was necessary to have peace, good health, and wealth. West Africans believed that natural events and animals gave them signs that allowed them to see into the future.

The creatures West Africans shared their land with and the land itself inspired many traditional beliefs.

Ancestors played a very important part in the religion and daily lives of West Africans. It was thought that ancestors stood between gods and the living and helped them speak with each other. A very strong tradition of family meant that West Africans were never alone and were always surrounded by relatives.

A West African symbol for God in heaven

The king determined the religion of his kingdom, and West Africans believed he was a god. The king did not walk directly on the ground because it was thought the king's feet would burn the earth! People were not even allowed to see their king eat.

West Africans buried their kings in a special forest where only priests could go. A huge wooden dome was built over the grave, and the king's body was carried on a covered bed and placed inside the dome. Clothing, weapons, possessions, vessels for eating and drinking, and even those who served him his food were left in the house for the king's use in the afterlife. Then the door was closed, and the dome was covered with mats and earth until it became a large burial mound.

West African religion was celebrated with song, dance, and prayers to the gods. One of the sacred times for ceremonies was autumn, when West Africans sacrificed animals in hopes for wealth in the coming year. Also, the birth of babies, the time when boys reached manhood, and marriages were observed. For these celebrations, wonderful masks and headdresses were carved of wood, hammered of iron, and sometimes made of a combination of materials. These masks and headdresses were believed to be direct connections to the spirit world. The more powerful they looked, the more effective they were believed to be.

Powerful-looking masks were believed to connect people to the spirit world.

Between 600 and 700 C.E., Arab ways of life spread throughout the West African Kingdoms. Muslims hoped the people would give up all their gods and accept one god, Allah. Many of the kings practiced both religions to keep the peace, but West Africans outside of the cities continued their traditional beliefs.

CHAPTER VIII:

THE PEOPLE TODAY

For decades West Africans struggled to gain their independence. They have been ruled by Great Britain, France, Belgium, Portugal, and Spain, but today they are a group of independent nations. The region once known as the Kingdoms of Ghana, Mali, and Songhay are parts of present-day Mauritania, Mali, Gambia, Guinea, Senegal, Burkina Faso, Benin, and Niger.

Most of the people in the region are Muslims who speak Arabic, while some people speak French. Black Africans belong to many different ethnic groups or clans and have their own languages. Large numbers of people live in modern cities, but those who live in rural areas still honor traditional customs and beliefs.

Crops such as dates, bananas, coffee, corn, peanuts, pineapples, plantains, rice, and sweet potatoes are grown and exported. The region continues to mine iron ore, gold, diamonds, and uranium. Building materials, food, machinery, petroleum products, transportation equipment, and consumer goods are some of the goods imported.

The geography of the area influences the Sahel lifestyle. In the desert areas, **nomads** live in tents and move over the desert with their cattle in search of water. Rural farmers live along the Senegal and Niger rivers in their circular houses still made of sun-dried brick. Most families raise only enough food to feed their families. Droughts can lead to famine and the deaths of people and animals.

Unlike the wealth of the ancient kingdoms, most sections of these countries are poor, with very little fertile soil. Mineral and water resources remain undeveloped. Most of the people cannot read or write. Children are required to finish at least six years of school, but very few actually attend school.

Clothing is traditional and loose fitting for comfort. Men wear floor-length gowns with long armholes over baggy trousers. Women wear **caftans** as well, but more often they wear a blouse and **faneau**, which is a piece of cloth tied at the waist to form a skirt. Women wear brightly colored jewelry and fancy turbans on their heads. Children are dressed like the adults, and sandals are common.

Islamic and traditional beliefs are both practiced. The chief of the Songhay clans is still considered to be an earthly form of god. He wears a **fula**, or hat of inner strength, and carries a wooden cane. The chief rarely speaks, except through a third party.

For centuries West Africa was a rich region. The Sahel provided the world with art, labor, and natural resources that brought attention to the cultures of West Africa. Vast mineral deposits, fossil fuels, and commercial crops came from the area. Some believe that the origins of all human beings started in Africa. Yet, the same challenges are present today that existed in the past. The rulers of each country face the difficult task of uniting many ethnic groups and different languages into a single state.

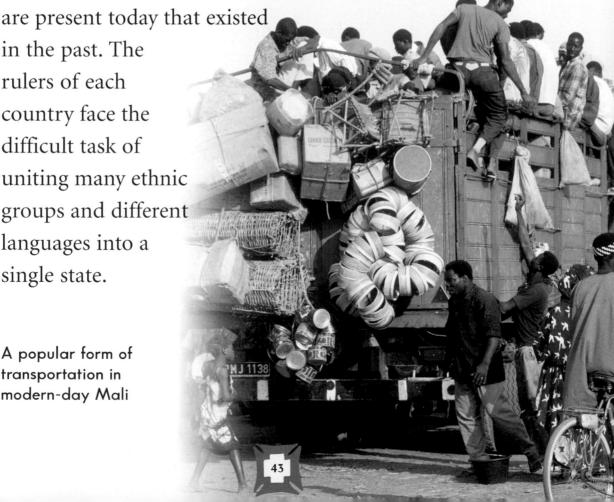

A popular form of transportation in modern-day Mali

A TIMELINE OF THE HISTORY OF THE
WEST AFRICAN KINGDOMS

300-500 C.E.	The empire of Ghana begins to emerge.
700 C.E.	The Soninke people start building Kumbi Saleh.
800-1000 C.E.	Ghana controls the gold and salt trade.
1076 C.E.	The Almoravids defeat Ghana and the kingdom of Mali emerges.
1235 C.E.	Sundiata unites kingdoms and forms Mali.
1235-1500 C.E.	Mali rules trade routes.
1312-1337 C.E.	Mansa Musa rules Mali.
1324 C.E.	Mansa Musa makes a pilgrimage to Mecca.
1433 C.E.	Enemies capture Timbuktu, and Mali grows weak.

1464-1591 C.E.	Songhay Empire controls trade routes.
1464 C.E.	Sonni Ali becomes king of Songhay.
1493 C.E.	Mohammed Askia comes to power as king of Songhay.
1591 C.E.	Moors fight and defeat Songhay.

Men in traditional Muslim dress in front of a mosque

GLOSSARY

Allah - The one god of Islam.

Balaphon - A musical instrument that uses dried gourds to increase the volume.

Berber - A member of a light-skinned, Muslim group of people from northern Africa.

Caftan - A full-length tunic or robe for men, usually made of rich fabric.

Caravan - Group of camels and traders.

C.E. - A time period beginning with the year of Christ's birth that is also known as Common Era or Christian Era.

Clan - A group of people with a common ancestor.

Cowrie - Type of shell sometimes used as money by ancient West Africans.

Dinar - A gold coin.

Discus - A weighted disk used in track and field games by an athlete who spins with arms out to throw the disk from the flat of his or her hand.

Empire - A group of countries under one ruler.

Epic - A long story or poem about the adventures and battles of a king, god, or hero.

Faneau - A piece of cloth tied at the waist to form a skirt.

Fula - Hat (symbol) of office.

Geometric - Decorative use of simple lines and shapes, especially on pottery.

Griot - A West African storyteller who passes on the history of a people through epics.

Hajj - The pilgrimage to Mecca, Saudi Arabia, that is required at least once in a Muslim's lifetime.

Islam - A religion that teaches that Allah is the one God.

Javelin - A spear thrown as a weapon or in games.

Jihad - Holy war to convert others to Islam.

Kante - West African clan whose special jobs were to be blacksmiths.

Kingdom of Ghana - Ancient West African kingdom between 700-1076 C.E.

Kingdom of Mali - Ancient West African kingdom between 1235-1433 C.E.

Kingdom of Songhay - Ancient West African kingdom between 1464-1591 C.E.

Kola nut - Nut containing caffeine.

Koran - The sacred text of Islam, also spelled Qu'ran.

Korte - Magic charm.

Mandinka - People of West Africa who built the Mali Empire. They are also called Maninka, Mandingo, or Manding.

Manatee - A mammal of tropical waters with a flat, rounded tail; sometimes called a sea cow.

Mecca - The birthplace of Muhammad and holy city of Islam. Muslims believe they should travel to Mecca at least once in their lifetimes.

Minarets - Slender towers with balconies.

Monkey Bread - Gourd-shaped fruit of the baobab tree. The pulp is eaten by monkeys and humans.

Moors - A mixture of people, mostly Arabs and Berbers, who lived in northern Africa.

Mosque - A Muslim building of worship.

Muslim - A person whose religion is Islam.

Nomads - People who have no fixed place to live and move from place to place within an area when the season changes or in search of food.

Oasis - Fertile ground of land in the desert where plants grow and travelers can refill their water supplies.

Pilgrimage - A trip to a holy place for a religious reason. This is called a hajj in Islam.

Plantain - A green fruit resembling a banana, eaten cooked as a staple food in many tropical countries.

Province - A division of a country controlled by an administrator.

Purdah - The traditional Muslim practice of keeping women fully covered with clothing and apart from the rest of society.

Ramadan - An annual Islamic fasting period.

Sahara - Largest desert in the world, covering nearly all of northern Africa. Total area of 3,320,000 sq miles (8,600,00 sq km).

Sahel - Region lying between the Sahara Desert and the forest lands to the south.

Shaduf - A water-raising device used in ancient Egypt.

Soninke - West African people who are known for building the Kingdom of Ghana.

Sorghum - Edible grain or cereal.

Tariff - A tax charged on goods that are brought into or carried out of a country.

Tribute - A payment made by a group of people to their ruler.

Turban - A traditional Muslim headdress consisting of a long scarf wrapped around the head.

Books of Interest

Armentrout, David and Patricia. *Ghana, Mali, & Songhay*. Florida: Rourke Publishing, 2004.

Adeleke, Tunde. *Songhay*. New York: Rosen Publishing Group, Inc., 1996.

Quigley, Mary. *Ancient West African Kingdoms: Ghana, Mali, & Songhai*. Chicago: Heinemann Library, 2002.

Nelson, Julie. *West African Kingdoms*. Texas: Steck-Vaughn Company, 2002.

Nwanumobi, C.O. *Soninke*. New York: The Rosen Publishing Group, 1996.

Thompson, Carol. *The Empire of Mali*. New York: The Rosen Publishing Group, Inc., 1998.

Web Sites

http://www.artnetweb.com/guggenheim/africa/sahelsav.html

http://www.metmuseum.org/toah/hd/ghan/hd_ghan.htm

http://www.vmfa.state.va.us/mali_geo_hist.html

INDEX

Almoravids 15

Atlantic Ocean 5, 6

Berbers 10

clans 8, 9, 10, 12

Djenne 6, 18, 23, 34

Gao 6, 18, 20, 21, 34

Ghana, Kingdom of 4, 5, 6, 10, 11, 12, 13, 14, 15, 16, 32, 41

griots 9, 36

Islam 15, 16, 19, 20, 22, 24, 25, 36, 37, 43

Kante (clan) 12

Koran 15, 19, 36

Kumbi Saleh 11, 12

Mali, Kingdom of 4, 5, 6, 16, 17, 18, 19, 20, 21, 23, 32, 36, 41

Mandinka 16, 17, 22

Mansa Musa 18, 19, 20

Mecca 18, 19, 25

Mohammed Askia 24, 25, 26, 27

Muhammad 16

Muslim 12, 15, 16, 17, 18, 20, 22, 24, 36, 37, 40, 41

Niani 16, 19, 21

Niger River 6, 7, 10, 16, 17, 20, 22, 28, 34, 42

Sahara Desert 5, 6, 13, 20, 32

Sahel 5, 7, 42, 43

Senegal River 6, 42

Songhay, Kingdom of 4, 5, 7, 20, 21, 22, 26, 27, 37, 41, 43

Soninke 6, 10, 11, 13, 22

Sonni Ali (king) 22, 23, 24

Sundiata Keita 16, 17, 18, 36

Takrur 6

Timbuktu 18, 23, 25, 31, 34

Wagadou 10, 14

Katherine E. Reece is a native of Georgia, where she grew up in a small town located in the foothills of the Blue Ridge Mountains. She has traveled throughout the United States, Europe, Australia, and New Zealand. Katherine completed her Bachelor of Fine Arts with an emphasis in studio art at the University of Colorado in Boulder, Colorado, where she now resides. Her extensive studies in art history gives her an appreciation for all that can be learned about the culture, beliefs, and traditions of ancient civilizations from the architecture, artifacts, and recordings that have been preserved through the centuries.